The ROLE of WOMEN

in Making Effective Disciples for Christ

by Henrietta C. Ekekezie

The ROLE of WOMEN *in Making Effective Disciples for Christ*
Copyright © 2018 by Henrietta C. Ekekezie

All rights reserved solely by the author. The author guarantees all contents are original and do not infringe upon the legal rights of any other person or work. No part of this book may be reproduced, stored in a retrieval system, or transmitted in any form or by any means without expressed written permission of the author. Thank you for your support of the author's rights.

Scriptures are from the Holy Bible, King James Version, Copyright © 1972 by Thomas Nelson Inc., Camden, New Jersey 08103.

Certain pronouns capitalized in Scripture that refer to the Father, Son and Holy Spirit is the author's choice as well as emphasis within Scripture quotations.

www.RefreshingGloryMinistries.org

ISBN: 978-1-7321597-0-9

Library of Congress in Publication Data

Category: Self-Help / Motivational & Inspirational / Faith / Women in Christ / Disciple Making

---

Written by: Henrietta C. Ekekezie | info@refreshinggloryministries.org

Edited by: Jahshua E. Blyden

Cover Design & Formatted by: Eli Blyden | CrunchTime Graphics *for Publishing*

Printed in the United States of America by: A&A Printing & Publishing

Dedication

To my Refreshing Glory Ministries Family and many other women, desiring to understand their role in making effective disciples for Christ and positively impact their generation.

The ROLE of WOMEN *in Making Effective Disciples for Christ*

Table of Contents

Dedication iii
Foreword vii
Introduction
Overview of a Disciple 13

CHAPTER ONE
What Does Making Disciples Mean to You?..................... 15

CHAPTER TWO
Who Is Qualified to Make Disciples? 21

CHAPTER THREE
When and Where Should We Make Disciples? 23

CHAPTER FOUR
Why Should We Make Disciples? 27

CHAPTER FIVE
How Should We Make Disciples? 29

CHAPTER SIX
The Role of Women in Making Effective Disciples for Christ 35

CHAPTER SEVEN
The Cost of Making Effective Disciples 45

CHAPTER EIGHT
The Benefits of Making Effective Disciples 49

CONCLUSION
Small Group Use Helpful Hints: 53
Wisdom: The Voice of Value *54*
The Epiphany! 55

DAILY AFFIRMATIONS
The Extraordinary Woman 57
Acknowledgements 59
About the Author 61
How to Contact the Author 63
Also Written by Henrietta C. Ekekezie 64

Foreword

I deem it a privilege to have been asked by a serious disciple of Jesus, Reverend Henrietta Ekekezie to write this foreword to her book entitled, *"The Role of Women in Making Effective Disciples for Christ"*. Rev. Ekekezie is a powerful woman of God. She continues to be a learner and student of the Holy Bible. She knows the Word of God. The Word of God is in her heart. The Word of God is actualized in her touching the lives of people daily. She is a true disciple of Jesus Christ.

I have known Rev. Ekekezie for several years. I have found her to be a true living vessel available to be used by the Lord Jesus Christ. She has been gifted in the areas of being a powerful preacher, administrator, teacher and writer, etc. I have experienced the Holy Ghost moving in a powerful way, touching the hearts of women and men in one of her Women's Conferences. She does not believe in being a lukewarm Christian. She believes one should give their services to the one who provides perpetual care, namely Jesus. She believes in Excellency in Ministry.

Rev. Ekekezie is a Prayer Warrior. She is known specifically as an Intercessor. Her intercessory prayer life renders positive results. I am a recipient of having this Intercessor to pray for my husband, family and myself. She is a faithful Prayer Warrior who calls on my Women's Prayer Conference Call Line every Wednesday morning. In my absence from the Prayer line, she takes the women prayer request and lead those women in prayer.

I am so excited that Rev. Ekekezie has been inspired by the Lord to write this book, *"The Role of Women in Making Effective Disciples for Christ."* This is a work that will not only bless women, but will also bless men. This work gets to the very heart of whom we are called to become. In our churches we are called to move from membership to discipleship. Rev. Ekekezie doesn't give the mandate from God for us to make disciples. She is a disciple of the Lord Jesus Christ. She is not selfish. She gives of herself untiringly. She gives hope in the midst of hopeless situations. She gives love to the least, the last and the almost forgotten.

Rev. Ekekezie is a gift from God to the body of Christ. I thank God for how she has impacted my life through prayer and words of encouragement. She is a powerful disciple of Jesus Christ. I pray that you will not only read this book, but use it as a resource in helping others to become effective disciples for Jesus Christ.

    Bishop Eunice T. Turner
    Bishop At Large
    International Evangelism College of Bishops

The ROLE of WOMEN *in Making Effective Disciples for Christ*

The ROLE of WOMEN
in Making Effective Disciples for Christ

Introduction

Overview of a Disciple

The term disciple, no doubt, is very familiar to most of us. According to Webster's Dictionary definition, a disciple is, "one who accepts and assists in spreading the doctrines of another." It involves the person teaching and modeling the ways of another he or she admires or believes in. When we relate it to Christianity, as in this context, a disciple means a dedicated follower of Jesus Christ. The desire to follow Him is borne out of your love for Him and wanting to see your life formed by His way of life. This love now passionately drives you to make disciples for Him, as you relentlessly share the tremendous impact He has had and continues to have in your life.

CHAPTER ONE

What Does Making Disciples Mean to You?

Making disciples for Christ can mean different things to different people. For some, it might mean witnessing to people and leading them to Christ and they become saved. To another, it could mean bringing them to Christ, and also helping them grow in the Word of God, to become mature believers. However, whatever our perspectives are in what making disciples mean, it is important we align our thoughts to the thoughts of Jesus Christ, who initiated this process. He has commissioned us to go into all nations, teaching them to observe, all that He has commanded us (See Matthew 28: 18-20). It's one thing to make disciples, but it is a *better* thing to make disciplined and effective disciples or followers. What it means to you will drive your level of commitment, and the quality of teaching and impact these lives. Do you realize that "making" is a process, and as such will require time? Every process involves several steps taken, in order to accomplish the goal. Making disciples, accordingly, is similar, as it is not a fast food drive - through, with an instant ready to - go meal. It is also not a *king* and his *subjects'* relationship, where the one discipling the others look down on them or feel superior to them. This line of thought may reveal a lack of understanding, on the purpose for which it was established by Christ. Don't be too far from the people you are trying to build up. Jesus never was. He was a lover of men. Notice that some of the discipling tools you will need are Prayer, the Word and Love of and for God. Discipling will involve living life with the people you are reaching; showing them love in your relationship with them; praying for them; teaching them the Word and many more. Like we know, leading people in any form is a *privilege given by the people being led, and not a right.* Effort should be made not to abuse it as, it is a great opportunity, love and honor, when people allow you to disciple them. Being wise in the approach seemingly, is vital, as every small beginning, has *genius* in them, and we also learn from one another. According to the book of John, all men will know we are His disciples, when we walk in love. (See John 17:35).

Now, have you considered that this process might require refocusing your priorities, so as to be intentional about disciple making? Have you pondered on how to transition "saved" people to "disciples," so that they can mature in their walk with God and train others? This training could be formal or informal. Note that some of the people that have influenced our lives informally, for instance, at home with our parents, are also part of this process. This might shock you. Has it ever occurred to you that disciples make disciples, but *only disciplined disciples or followers, can make disciplined and effective disciples?* Are you one? If you are, what type of disciple are you? Are you a disciplined and effective follower? Recall for a moment that Jesus Christ was a disciplined and effective follower of His Heavenly Father. Why did He follow Him every step of the way? I imagine that His conscious effort to follow, helped Him acquire the necessary skills, wisdom and understanding needed, to fulfill His purpose on the earth. Remember, whatever is put into these, will ultimately manifest. Have you also reflected on the different types of people we are actually discipling, and their make up? I will like to paint a picture here, to enable the understanding of what we are getting into, when embarking on the process of making disciples.

Imagine you go fishing for men in a river, or an ocean (life's ocean - the world), with a *sea of men*, using the Word of God as the "bait." You will notice that when you *go*, as *commanded*, to all nations and *catch* them, for instance in Africa, Asia, Australia, Antarctica, Europe, North and South America (*the seven continents of the globe),* or even from just a few, *most* of them might have characteristics that are as varied as the fishes in the ocean. "Salmons" differ from 'Tilapias" as well as "Mackerels". So does the "mix" you might have. This means, you may be "loaded" with people with different thoughts, values, lifestyles and many more. Can you now see clearly what discipling might mean for you, such as, some challenges that might lie ahead, with the blend you might have? Do you now begin to see that, if you are going to make disciples, it will require more effort on your part to grow in the overwhelming love of God? Consciously developing this love walk will help you to graciously overcome, the "hiccoughs" that may be experienced along the way, and still be able to give your best in the undertaking. Making disciples, undoubtedly, means a lot more; a lot more of His grace; a lot more of His love; a lot more of His patience, joy, wisdom and peace, to stay through the process.

Making disciples also means preparing to develop and answer a lot of questions. You cannot make effective disciples if you are not knowledgeable of the Word of God. It is a must-study. You can't teach what you don't know. As a growth tool, there will be questions from the one discipling and those being discipled. Questioning or asking questions is the foundation of anything in life. You can go from a novice to a genius, and a new believer to a matured Christian, through questioning. The great thing about this is that it helps you to study more. As you study, you learn; as you learn, you grow; as you grow, you change; as you change, you make progress, mature and become all that God wants you to be. Most importantly, you become agents of change, through living out the principles and values of the kingdom in your generation, thus bringing absolute glory to our God.

Overall, making disciples for Christ will mean, teaching believers that they are saved, not just to go to heaven, but to fulfill kingdom purposes here on earth, hence, will need to be equipped with the kingdom principles, values and lifestyle, to become positive agents of change in their world, and bring unending glory to God.

CHAPTER TWO

Who Is Qualified to Make Disciples?

It will not be improper for anyone to ponder if it is not out of place to ask this question, since every Christian can and should make disciples? I am aware of this perspective however; it will be beneficial for us to attempt to look at the big picture. Life has taught us, time and time again, that we cannot give what we don't have; we cannot teach or share what we don't know and that we reproduce who we are. This being said, it implies that the quality of those to make these disciples, matter, as they will teach, represent and reflect the kingdom values and principles desired, to make others want to be a part of it.

Reflecting on who Jesus was, when He was here on earth reveals some of the qualifications of those, who may desire, to be involved in making disciples. Was He not an embodiment of love, humility and discipline? He walked the "talk" and thus, multiplied or duplicated Himself in His disciples. His discipline produced effective disciples or followers. They could trust Him because He was integral with the words He spoke. Humility, love and discipline should be very fundamental to the core of anyone desiring to engage in this process. Firstly, love of God and love for God propels you to go, while humility and discipline enables you to stay through the process. Disciples make disciples, but only disciplined followers can make effective disciples, that will become agents of change, and transform their world. According to 2Timothy 2:2, *"And the things that thou hast heard of me among many witnesses, the same commit thou to faithful men, who shall be able to teach* others also." In other words, those qualified to make effective disciples, are qualified to be multiplied, as they will produce quality kingdom fruits.

CHAPTER THREE

When and Where Should We Make Disciples?

Some of us I'm sure may now be thinking, I truly desire to be a force in making disciples, but my time is so choked up that I don't know how to build in additional time to commit to this process. Others may also be wondering where exactly to go and start making disciples. No matter what your concerns or questions are, know that you are not in this all by yourself. God is with you. He sees your heart and knows where you are. Remember, God will never lead you to where His grace cannot sustain you. Do you know that as much as it will be a good thing to commit to a set time in making disciples, so as to have structure, it could still be done outside a set time or a church setting? If someone is unable to come to church to be discipled, does that mean they should be left out in this process? My point is that discipling can be done anywhere, so long as it is done well. Do you also know you can make and build disciples wherever you are? People can be discipled at home, church, school, your work place or anywhere you can reach them and is convenient to the parties involved. Realize that God has assigned a purpose for you each day and think of what you can do to seize the moment. He will never abandon you.

We can also make disciples while living life. By this I mean, we can make and build disciples by paying attention to what is already there. Say you go and work out with an acquaintance at the gym daily, you can ask him or her questions to see the opportunity you may have to share the love of God, and subsequently, lead them and build them up in Christ. You can also use different methods in your approach and settings. It could be formal or informal settings; a one-on-one or group settings. Jesus Christ was very creative in the ways He reached out to people and built them up. Let's not forget we are made in His image and in His likeness. In His image, we look like Him. In His likeness, we function like Him. If He is creative, so are we. We have that ability and capability. All we need to do is to tap into the power of who we are in Him, and we will see His enabling grace and power helping us to reach others anywhere and anytime. The purpose is for us to genuinely share with them what Christ has taught and commanded us, not our opinions or life convictions that are not backed up by the Word of God. Breakfast meetings, luncheons, dinner, picnics, tea parties, lunch and learn fellowships and many more, are some great settings to initiate this Christ - relationship building process, through discipling making.

CHAPTER FOUR

Why Should We Make Disciples?

Our asking why we should make disciples is like asking, "Why should we make lawyers, nurses, physicians, accountants and many more?" Numerous societal benefits, we are aware, emanate from that workforce and their services. Making disciples for Christ is also not an exception, as it also helps us to raise kingdom people, to fulfill kingdom purposes, through learning its principles, values and way of life, and model it wherever they may go on this earth. I think a better question will be, "Why should we not make disciples?" If Jesus Christ did it to accomplish His Kingdom purposes, why not us? Not doing so will mean we will not get His results. Let's remind ourselves for a moment that we are not the initiators of this process. He is. He knows the inherent benefits in making disciples more than us. Perhaps, if He never made disciples, who knows, He may never have accomplished all that He did within that short space of time. Disciples are crucial for growing the kingdom. No one disciple can succeed in extending the kingdom of God here on this earth. Making disciples means raising up *ambassadors of Christ* (See 2 Corinthians 5:20); people that know and understand the tenets of His kingdom and know how to uphold it. You cannot represent someone you don't know their values or principles. We can't say we are following Him and we build in our own methods and principles. If we truly are imitating Him, we ought to follow His every step.

I also believe that part of the confusion in not making effective disciples or disciplined followers of Christ is the lack of clarity in the purpose, and why we do it. It is important we know firstly that, it is the will of God for us to make disciples. In the book of Matthew, we see where Jesus Christ authorized His disciples to do so (See Matthew 28:18-20). Secondly, we ought to know and understand what is in it for us. My perspective is, if we know we will get paid, we definitely, will go to work. Therefore, if those who ought to make disciples know and understand their priceless value in establishing kingdom principles, through investing their time in teaching and building up others, to ultimately glorify God in the earth, they will make disciples, and intentionally too.

CHAPTER FIVE

How Should We Make Disciples?

It is difficult to teach someone how to make a dish of fried rice when you have never been taught, nor shown the process, nor have actually made one by yourself. The same thing is applicable to the "how" of making disciples, as it involves process. The truth of the matter is that no one person is an expert in making disciples. Often in life, we step into some areas we are initially not comfortable with, but as we go along with determination, perseverance and also an open mind to teach, and to be taught, we realize before midway that we are actually coasting along very well, and enriching many lives as well as ourselves. Here's my point, we don't have to know every process of discipling before doing so. Many things we might think we have a grip on, may confront us in a different way in the process. Realizing ahead of time we may not know what to do in the circumstance, will require total reliance on the one who has sent us, to lead and guide us every step of the way. Now let's look at a few steps in the "how" of making disciples:

Teaching:

Teaching is one of the fundamental methods of empowering disciples. They are not only taught the values of the kingdom but also to obey them. They learn through teaching, but are also given a voice, as they are able to give a constructive feedback, on the benefits of the process. The whole essence is to understand, assimilate the kingdom values and principles, to make a difference in their world. Through teaching they not only learn, but are motivated to share their new passion, and live a life, reflective of the kingdom.

Be a Point of Reference:

Be a version of what you are teaching. Show them the lifestyle of the kingdom This may be funny, but the reality is that people usually don't do what you say, they do what you do. Don't make people say of you that who you are, actually speaks so loudly, that they cannot hear what you are saying.

Correction:

In every teaching or training, there is a learning curve for both the teacher and the student. This usually happens when there is an obvious lack of understanding, and proper demonstration of what had been taught prior. Do you recall when Jesus Christ rebuked His disciples, when they could not cast out the devil in a little boy child? He was openly frustrated with them for not being able to do that, having been with Him for so long. He now reiterated to them that this type of sickness would not go away, but by prayer and fasting (See Matthew 17:17-21). Yes, He rebuked them, but in the rebuke was an inherent lesson for the disciples, regarding their kingdom assignment. The same principle should be emulated when discipling Christians today. Show them their error; teach them again, so they can become better.

Love

You cannot be a disciple maker if your love "tank" is always running on low. The "Jesus" we are imitating and following, was a lover of men. We cannot say we are imitating Him and are incapable of extending love to another. John 13:35 says, "By this, shall all men know that you are my disciples, if you have love, one to another." The whole essence of making disciples is predicated on the love of and for God. Love is the propelling force to go make disciples of all nations.

Humility:

Pride has never been a positive force in any relationship, and it is certainly not a healthy infusion, in the process of making disciples. Since we are the keepers of the legacy of Jesus Christ, it is important for us to align our actions to reflect His tenets. As He was humble, so should we be. It may not be easy, but His enabling grace is sufficient to steer us towards the right direction. Humility endears one to people, but pride is a turn off. In our journey of making disciples, may we adorn ourselves with the beauty of humility, to enable us to fulfill the kingdom mandate.

Courage:

It's not enough to ask, "How should we make disciples?" It is crucial we receive strength and courage to engage in the process. We can know every detailed process, but without courage, we may never step into our purpose to bring unending glory to our God. Let's challenge ourselves and rise to the occasion.

CHAPTER SIX

The Role of Women in Making Effective Disciples for Christ

The call to make disciples for Christ, no doubt, is to every believer. Women, therefore, are no exception. However, as a woman, have you ever paused to consider or reflect on what your role is, in making disciples for Christ? Firstly, what does making disciples for Christ mean to you as a woman? Do you even acknowledge you have a role, responsibility or a relevant part to play in the disciple making process? If your answer is in the affirmative, what will be your driving motive to engage in this vision process? Are you a disciple? What type of disciple are you? Are you a disciplined follower or a "zigzag" follower of Christ? In all honesty, are you truly convinced you are even, a disciple? Do you realize that when you disciple others, you are duplicating yourself? Is who you are now, worthy of duplication in another? Don't forget that in life, we reproduce who we are! Earnestly ask yourself, who are you, where are you, who should you be discipling and for what purpose do you want to disciple them? Any time frame attached to this process? Will it be worth your time and effort to be part of this? What is in it for you? Will the benefits of being a disciple and making other disciples for Christ outweigh not engaging in it? Do you think you will avert living a "driven" life and step right into a God directed life, by participating in this process?

It's never too late to do the right thing. It's never too late to engage in the process of discovering who you are, to understand your role, how to function with yourself, as well as with others. Your discovery will also equip you in knowing the strategy to adopt, in the execution of your role functions. Do you know you can be significant and still not know who you are, nor your role, responsibility or the part you are supposed to play, in this disciple making process? You are not alone, I can assure you, in this confusion of identity and role crisis. Do you realize that Queen Esther did not know who she was, or her role as a queen? It took her uncle, Mordecai, to wake her up to know what "time" it was for her people - the Jews, at the time. They were facing annihilation, when Mordecai sent people to her to go and plead with her husband, the king, to spare the Jews from being destroyed completely. Queen Esther's response to her uncle was that, it was not a good time for her to go and meet with the king, as she could be killed in the process. Mordecai was adamant and told her, "Who knows, maybe that's why you have come to the kingdom, for such a time as this?" Queen Esther on hearing this, now staggered out of her stupor, moved quickly into action, called her maids to join her to fast for three days, before going to see the king, and consequently, obtained his favor to stop the plot of killing the Jews. (See Esther 4 & 5). Here's my point, Esther, a queen, did not have an understanding of who she actually was, nor the influence she wielded in the land, and almost missed the purpose of her being a queen, at that particular time, had she not acted promptly. I'm saying all this to say that, Esther, I believe, became a queen, not just because of her beauty, but more due to the purpose ordained for her by God, to be the instrument of deliverance for her people. I'm realizing daily that ignorance can rob people of things they deserve or belong to them. It almost robbed Esther, a queen! Is it not sad to think for one moment that, Queen Esther only thought she was a mere object of beauty for the king, his decorated queen, and not one with dignifying influences, to change the course of her nation? Knowing who we are, to know our role, is crucial to making effective disciples and even in other areas of life.

Now, when we know who we are and what our role is, the next thing is to ask ourselves, "Where are we at?" Yes, we may know who we are and our roles, but do we know where we are at in terms of the role we are supposed to be playing? Are we acquainted with or trained and ready to assume the role assigned to us? Are we still guessing on what our role or responsibility should be, or do we want to properly understand and engage in this role, by educating ourselves and strategizing on how to acquire necessary skills, to be our best in this role? Are we open to reach out to those who may know more, to help us develop and fine-tune the skills needed, to enjoy the journey of making effective disciples? Let's also not forget to engage the tool of prayer, which is very significant in making this process a success.

Now let's explore some of the roles of women, in making effective disciples for Christ:

- Ambassadors for Christ

One of the fundamental roles of women in making effective disciples for Christ is to represent Him in word, thought and deed. What we say, think or do should be a reflection of the one we are following, and sharing with others. In other words, one of the roles is to raise the kingdom standard in our generation. Be the Jesus you share. This we cannot accomplish in our own strength rather, through developing a continuous relationship with Him, we can do all things, because He is the one that strengthens us to do so.

- Be Integrity - Driven

People do what we do, not what we say or tell them to do. Being integral with our word will make people believe in what we are sharing with them thus, making us trustworthy. If we don't practically show what we are saying in our relationship with others, making disciples will be very difficult or almost impossible. Always remember we are His representative and model Him.

- Be Consistent

No one likes to follow someone that is inconsistent. Our role should be to bring stability in areas that are unstable, through our examples. Say you are leading a group of women, and you schedule a meeting for 10:00am, your goal should be to get there at least 10 minutes before the start time. This will encourage the others in the next meeting, to get there earlier too. Consistently not coming in on time, might be perceived as indifference to the purpose for which the meeting has been convened. Some observing this as a pattern may never come again, as people value their time. Our commitment level will determine the quality and the effectiveness of those we are discipling. It's often said that, "like begets like." Realize that making disciples is not only when we go outside of our church, get people saved and start discipling them. Many already are in church or our sphere of influence needing to be discipled. Begin where you are; help equip them with the principles and values of the kingdom, through teaching and modeling His life in all we do. As a matter of fact, we are the "little Jesus" they are seeing and following. Don't be a "zigzag" disciple maker, as it will frustrate those assigned to you. Be a disciplined and effective follower in your role, and others will emulate you.

- Add Your Flavor

Women naturally make good dishes for their families. Why? I think it's because they know already the type of food they want to prepare. They have mastery of the ingredients required; the right portions to add; when to add them; where to add them; how long to let them cook, simmer or bake. They know their expected end result. Same process is applicable to making effective disciples. What end result are we looking at, for the people we are discipling? Are we seeing them in their future or are we still seeing them in their today? Realize that, just as time is needed to prepare a good meal; gathering the right ingredients and adding them when necessary, time also will produce a disciplined and effective disciple, through adequate training and teaching of kingdom values and principles. The wisdom to know when, where and how to introduce these principles, is what makes the difference. Life has shown that, it's not what we say to people that makes or breaks them, it is how we say it that matters. It's time to bring our natural gifting and flavor into this area of making disciples. See every disciple as a unique "dish." Prepare and seek wisdom on how to make a "good kingdom dish" out of this person. Ask God for wisdom through His Word to know when to teach, encourage, correct, listen or guide them in the disciple making process. Bringing correction to a disciple, when what they need at the time is encouragement, can lead to a broken fellowship. Know your role. Know your goal. *Knowing your role will help you know your goal.* Be driven by the privilege of being part of the making of kingdom giants and agents of change, for the glory of God.

- Be Caring and Hospitable

Women are known to care for everyone around them, so, caring for disciples will not be out of place for them. Do you know that people know when we care? Saying we care does not mean we care. Naturally, we care for people we love. Are you a lover of people? In making disciples, do you have a culture of caring for one another? Are you selective in your care outreach? How much of your brother or sisters keeper are you? Women are nurturers and hospitable. Reflecting these qualities in your role in making disciples already makes you winners. The kingdom we are serving in is a kingdom of care. Our role model was the epitome of care.

People often say, love is a verb, and requires action to back it up. In this role, we need to let people know that we genuinely care through our love actions towards them. How do you weigh on the scale of showing care and being hospitable? Do you reach out to new and existing members periodically to know how they are doing? Are people you are discipling free to share their concerns with you because they know you genuinely care? Intentionally developing and enriching this aspect of your role will bring great results in the disciple - making process.

- Be Humble

Jesus, as great as He was, walked in humility. Is it not proper that we should reflect Him in this area? Do we have the prerogative to choose aspects of Him we should follow or not follow? When we are not walking in humility, who then are we representing? This truly is an area we need to make a very conscious effort not to do otherwise. Having the privilege of discipling people does not mean we are in any way better. Those discipling others are not "queens" or those being discipled, their "maids." It is the "Train the Trainers" kingdom program.

- Be Patient and Perseverance Driven

Staying through the challenges of the process to see the amazing results of harvest is very fulfilling. Marathon runners know the importance of patience and perseverance. They are two of the best tools for any success. They help you see the joy and reward that lies ahead, when kingdom giants are adequately trained.

They stretch your vision to see the destination, not the journey; the invisible and do the impossible! The road may not be easy, but it will be worth every time you put in, every sacrifice you made, when the big picture is ultimately realized.

I'm sure the insight of now knowing who you are and your role, has ignited your passion to go and serve the kingdom, with the honorable God - assigned role. Disciplined followers make effective disciples. Extraordinarily disciplined followers make extraordinarily effective disciples, and you can be one. It's time to go and manifest your glory, having been equipped with the tools and understanding, to make effective disciples, agents of change, and bring glory to God.

CHAPTER SEVEN

The Cost of Making Effective Disciples

In life, there is a cost to most of the things we do or desire to have. There's a cost to getting education and earning a degree, diploma, certificate or whatever we decide to be our chosen focus. Regarding putting food on our tables also, there is a cost to receiving the weekly, bi-weekly or monthly pay checks as the case may be, to enable us to take care of our daily needs. Making disciples also, is not an exception. In all of the afore-mentioned, they each require a decision on our part, to engage in the process, and make it a reality.

Time investment, is one of the inevitable costs in making disciples. Availability is critical. If we are not ready to create time for this process, I will say, maybe we are not ready yet. Why? I believe the investment of time needed in the disciple- making process is more of sharing ourselves, or spending our lives with them. We are the ones to teach them, guide them, be there for them when they are unsure of the next step to take along this chosen path. If we are not able to make out time for this, how can they grow to disciple another? I liken making disciples to raising a child. We take care of them, nourish and nurture them from babies to adults. It's quite a journey as it takes time and patience. Same thing is applicable with making disciples. It is not a "walk" in the park

Criticism is one of the many costs of making disciples. It is hard to please everyone, as there will always be those, who never see any good in your genuine efforts and sacrifice, no matter how hard you try. Knowing the obvious, how should you position yourself? I will recommend having a made - up mind to love, in spite of any opposition. The simple question to ask is, "What will Jesus do in the same scenario?" I believe that answering this question, ahead of time, will make you an enviable winner in this arena.

Strength depletion, is another area disciple making can affect, if proper balance is not maintained. The demands of scheduling growth - oriented meetings, one-on- ones, to know where each one is at, can take its toll on people, if not planned adequately. Suffice it to say that, discipline in every area is required, to achieve maximum success with the process.

CHAPTER EIGHT

The Benefits of Making Effective Disciples

Benefits imply, what is in it for me or you? If there's nothing in it for us, why should we bother engaging in it? However, like most of the things in life with many benefits, so is disciple making and below are just a few:

- Being Obedient to God's Command

We are doing the will of God, by making disciples as He did, and also commanded us. Our part in the process is to obey His instructions. His part is to make it come to fruition. According to the book of Corinthians, Paul planted, Apollos watered, but God gave the increase (See 1Corinthians 3:6-8).

- Cultivating a Deeper Love for People

When we have a better understanding and revelation of who God is, and His love for mankind, we desire to do the same knowing it is His heartbeat. John 3:16 says, "For God so loved the world that He gave His only begotten Son, that whosoever believeth in Him should not perish, but have everlasting life). God is not only a lover of people, He is love personified. Being made in His image and likeness, we ought to love and function like him,

- Helping People to Follow Jesus

The joy of teaching and helping people to mature in their Christian walk is very rewarding. It is a privilege to do so, thus adding value to the lives of many.

- Creating a Culture of Humility and Discipline

No disciple making process can be successful without developing a culture of humility and discipline. Humility strengthens the unity between the participants, while discipline is necessary to establish the boundaries and ensure progress.

- Building Up Effective Believers

Knowing who you are and your place in the kingdom is very vital to kingdom growth. Disciple making is an empowering process, that develops effective believers to become kingdom leaders and positive agents of change in their world.

CONCLUSION
Small Group Use Helpful Hints:

As making effective disciples is key to our kingdom mandate, it is important that we go about it intentionally. As a maturing tool, it requires quality time to be invested into the lives of people who are hungry and passionate about learning, and modeling the life of Christ. A well-trained disciple will ultimately be like the teacher. Furthermore, continued obedience to investing in them, will eventually evolve into meaningful and lasting relationships, that will sustain the work of the kingdom. Below are some of the hints:

- Build in time to socialize, pray together and strategize as best fits your setting, group and time frame.
- Create small teams of three or four women to enable intimate participation.
- Invite your groups to read the book ahead of time

- Develop 3-5 questions for each session (I recommend *one chapter* for each session)

- Set a date, time and place suitable to your groups to share their insights

- Test what you have gained by implementing *one new skill* in your disciple making strategy *each month*

- Develop a "question bank" from the teams. If you exhaust your prepared questions for the session before the meeting is over, you can pull from the bank. Getting every team member involved in developing the questions will make them not only accountable, but they will feel being a part of the solution process. In life, usually, whatever you commit to, you don't want it to fail.

Wisdom: The Voice of Value

Preparation precedes success, as nothing in life comes easy. True success is never an accident, so leave nothing to chance. Prepare to succeed in this undertaking, and success will follow. Make *prayer* your building block; let *love* be your emblem; be a *Word Practitioner* and never give up!

The Epiphany!

Realize that the work God has for you, has a commanding significance, which is worth your every sacrifice, to bring it to pass. This book unveils the hidden secrets and answers to your many questions, on your role and making disciples. It discloses that to know your role, requires knowing who you are, so as to properly function in the assigned role, and achieve the expected results. May this book be an epiphany, where the nuggets, already leaping off of the pages of this book, will help you in the discipling making process. Relentlessly embrace love, righteousness and peace, as you continue to teach kingdom values and principles to raise kingdom agents of change, and consequently, bring glory to God. In all that you do, always remember that, "You have been called, to raise the standard, in your generation!"

DAILY AFFIRMATIONS
The Extraordinary Woman

I am an Extraordinary WOMAN in Christ Jesus
I have Great Power
I will do Great Things in God
I see the Invisible
I believe the Impossible
I will do the Incredible
I have the Heart of a Champion
The mind of a Winner
And
I possess, the Spirit of a Conqueror!

Acknowledgements

Nothing enables success in life like the encouragement, support and influence from the family, friends and many more. Their continuous support helps make it easy for me to fulfill God's will.

A special thanks to Ambassador Marjorie R. Kornegay, for lending her editing skills as well as input to this project.

Bisi Oladipo, your make-up artistic skill evidenced in the book cover picture, made this book look better.

I would also like to thank Jahshua Blyden for his editorial expertise and insight into this work.

A special thanks to Eli Blyden and the entire CrunchTime Graphics team, for helping to make this book a success.

Last but not the least, thanks to Maryellen O'Rourke and A & A Printing, my publishing family, for the printing, publishing and production of this book.

About the Author

Henrietta C. Ekekezie
Author, Speaker, Empowerment Coach

Born in Nigeria, West Africa, Reverend Henrietta, is the President and Founder of Refreshing Glory Ministries Inc., a People Empowerment Ministry that is dedicated to developing, and empowering women from all nations, to reach their highest potential, through the vehicle of prayer. Her philosophy that, "where you are, is not who you are" encourages women to maximize their capabilities and attain quality growth spiritually, mentally, emotionally and physically. She is committed to helping invest women with power to become what they believe.

She is also a Prayer Intercessor, Teacher and Retreat/Conference Organizer.

Major facets of her ministry are: Power Prayer sessions, Bible Study Fellowships, Retreats and Empowerment Seminars and Outreaches where she offers quality teachings for effective spiritual growth. Her meetings are characterized with an atmosphere filled with the Refreshing Glory and Presence of God, inspiring people they are meant for more, and to actively discover their unique God-given purpose through seeking the wisdom of God in prayer. An additional component to her portfolio includes teaching and developing women to consciously cultivate, lead change that is Godly, through intentional growth and become what they believe. Through Refreshing Glory Ministries, she is extensively involved with other ministries where she serves on several committees. She is also the Vision Leader of SPIRITUAL KITCHEN, a vision that embraces women from all nations and works of life, coming together to intercede in prayer for all, and empower both young and old.

Some of her educational background include; Bachelor of Education degree with a major in English Language, Bachelor of Science degree in Nursing, and a Master of Science degree in Organizational Leadership.

How to Contact the Author

~

**Henrietta C. Ekekezie,
Founder - Refreshing Glory Ministries Inc.**

To reach the author regarding,
a speaking engagement,
future events - conferences, seminars, retreats,
empowerment coaching and outreaches,
or to read about her upcoming books and
other ministry products,

please visit her website at:
Web: www.refreshinggloryministries.org
Email: info@refreshinggloryministries.org
www.Facebook.com/RefreshingGloryMinistriesInc

Phone: *1-888-247-0478*

Or write to mailing address:
*10482 Baltimore Avenue Suite 114
Beltsville, MD 20705*

~

Also Written by Henrietta C. Ekekezie

www.ingramcontent.com/pod-product-compliance
Lightning Source LLC
Chambersburg PA
CBHW060429050426
42449CB00009B/2209